21 Days of Healing

A Journal for Healing & Hope

Copyright © 2020 by Isabel Rojas'Lopez
All rights reserved. This book or any portion thereof may not be reproduced or used in any manner whatsoever without the express written permission of the publisher except for the use of brief quotations in a book review.

Printed in the United States of America

First Printing, 2020

ISBN 9781655129049
Edited & Formatted by Show Your Success
Published by Isabel Rojas' Lopez

INTRODUCTION

The healing journey happens in many layers. It is individual and highly personal. I created *21 Days of Healing* as an interactive journal designed to guide you through your healing journey. Featuring 21 days of inspiring quotes, open-ended questions, and prompts to record your thoughts and emotions. This journal is a powerful tool for 21 days of healing and beyond. It's the ultimate safe space for your reasoning and emotions.

Remember, the path to healing starts with you.

THIS HEALING JOURNAL BELONGS TO

_____

"The emotion that can break your heart is sometimes the very one that heals it."

- *She Heals*
_____

"She believed she could, so she did"

- R.S. Grey

One of the greatest challenges I've overcome:

Three things I am scared to admit out loud and why:

NOTES

> **"Forward progress, just keep moving you got this."**
>
> *- Isabel Rojas' Lopez Author*

Day 2

Five things I am grateful for and why:

What is keeping me from living my life on my own terms?

What am I looking to heal from?

NOTES

"Rock bottom became a foundation on which I rebuild my life."

- J.K Rowling

Day 3

What am I most grateful for and why?

_____

_____

_____

_____

_____

_____

_____

_____

_____

_____

_____

_____

_____

_____

_____

_____

What are my top three fears? Which fear could I make more of an effort to overcome?

What would I gain if I released those fears? What would I lose?

NOTES

"We repeat what we don't repair."

- Christine Langley

Day 4

Change is a fact of life. In what way does change scare me and why?

_____

_____

_____

_____

_____

_____

_____

_____

_____

_____

_____

_____

_____

_____

When was the last time I felt totally exposed and vulnerable?

What are the two most important relationships in my life? If I am being honest with myself, to what extent am I being authentic in each of them?

NOTES

"Don't overlook your greatest healing tool, your intuition."

- Carol Harrington

Day 5

What parts of my life don't reflect who I am?

Where am I not being honest with myself and why?

Am I comfortable with being uncomfortable?

NOTES

"**Healing comes when we choose to walk away from darkness and move towards a brighter light.**"

- Dieter F. Unchtdorf

Day 6

What is the one thing I love most about myself?

What makes me happy?

What am I most passionate about?

NOTES

"Healing doesn't mean the damage never existed. It means the damage no longer controls our lives."

- Author unknown

Day 7

Do I love myself as much as I expect others to love me?

In what areas of my life am I trading authenticity for safety? Why?

Can I be alone without feeling lonely?

NOTES

"God help me to see the good in the 'not knowing' the joy in the 'in-between' and the meaning in the 'meantime.'"

- Spiritual inspirations

Day 8

Am I a good example for those around me?

Is the life that I am living the life I *want* to be living?

Do the people I surround myself with add value to my life?

NOTES

"The body heals with play, the mind heals with laughter and the spirit heals with joy."

- Proverb

Day 9

What are the top three feelings that are dominating my life?

If I could improve one aspect of my life, what would it be and why?

What have I been doing and continue to do in my life that I know is not working for me?

NOTES

"The soul always knows what to do to heal itself. The challenge is to silence the mind."

- Caroline Myss

Day 10

Am I harboring resentment towards others or myself?

What negative habits do I have that I need to work on?

What motivates me to heal?

NOTES

"She stood in the storm, and when the
wind did not blow her away,
she adjusted her sails."

- Elizabeth Edwards

Day 11

What am I most passionate about and would like to do more of in life?

What actions towards my healing journey do I need to prioritize?

The top three affirmations I will practice daily that will align me with my healing journey:

NOTES

―――――――――――――――――
"You are not a drop in the ocean. You are the entire ocean in a drop."

- Rumi
―――――――――――――――――

Day 12

What does self-improvement mean to me?

How do I see myself?

How do I want to be seen?

NOTES

**"I am better off healed than
I was unbroken."**

- Beth Moore

Day 13

What excites me about this healing journey?

What do I desire and want on this journey?

What is worthy of my attention?

NOTES

"Healing your past will free you to have the future you deserve."

- Unknown

Day 14

Top three priorities I will make to honor my healing:

How can I be empowered?

How can I find more meaning in my life?

NOTES

"I go beyond barriers to possibilities."

- Louise Hay

Day 15

What is the difference between living and existing?

If not now, then when?

What would I do different if I knew nobody would judge me?

NOTES

"We do not heal the past by dwelling there: We heal the past by living fully in the present."

- Mariane Williamson

Day 16

What makes me smile?

What does joy look like? What do I need to do to experience more of it?

When was the last time I tried something new? How did I feel?

NOTES

"Healing is not an overnight process. It is a daily cleansing of pain, it is a daily healing of your life."

- Leon Brown

Day 17

What does it mean to be vulnerable? Am I comfortable with being vulnerable? Why or why not?

What does inner peace mean to me? Why?

These are five things I will work on today that will bring me closer to experiencing inner peace:

NOTES

"Somehow in the midst of struggle, life finds its way to take care of you when you open yourself to receive healing and all will be well."

- Bella Bleue

Day 18

What would I like to stop worrying about? What steps can I take to let go of the worry?

_____

_____

_____

_____

_____

_____

_____

_____

_____

_____

_____

_____

_____

_____

How will I move past unpleasant thoughts or experiences?

What are my most important needs and desires?

NOTES

> "Sometimes what you're most afraid of doing is the very thing that will set you free."
>
> *- Unknown*

What are my personal strengths and gifts?

What three words describe me best?

NOTES

"When life brings big winds of change that almost blow you over, close your eyes, hang on tight, and believe."

- Winning Path

Day 20

How do I feel when I enforce my personal boundaries?

What makes me feel motivated, inspired and excited?

Do I feel seen, heard and validated? If not, how do I plan to change that?

NOTES

"**If you don't heal what hurt you, you'll bleed on people who didn't cut you.**"

- Unknown

Day 21

What does self-care mean to me?

If I wanted to find a place of sanctuary right now, where would I go? Why?

What is my biggest dream?

NOTES

"Healing is an art. It takes time, it takes practice, it takes love."

- Unknown

NOTE TO SELF

21 AFFIRMATIONS

I release any ways I feel responsible
I release trauma
I release low self-worth
I release worry
I release guilt
I release fear
I release turmoil
I release shame
I release self-doubt
I believe in myself
I clear all the ways I can't get relief from these thoughts
I am worthy of love
I am worthy of praise
I am enough
I trust myself, I know what's good for me
I am deserving of love and respect
I am a good person
I am loving, kind and a clear reflection of God
I am the author of my own destiny
I possess the strength to succeed
I love myself

MANTRA

"I am grateful for all that is unfolding in my life and all that is yet to come."

I am fulfilled

I am fearless

CREATE YOUR MANTRA

REFLECTIONS

Now that you have completed your 21 days of healing, you can easily recognize and practice the new habits you have created. Hopefully, this self-exploration has also brought you a greater sense of confidence and positivity. Once you have read and reviewed your entries, ask yourself these questions:

What are the top 3 significant changes I will make on this new journey?

What have I learned about myself?

Has my outlook on my past changed since I started keeping this journal? If so, in what ways?

Do I have unfinished business?

What inner work do I need to prioritize to heal?

By revisiting your journal entries, you might recognize some themes and patterns you did not recognize prior to picking up this journal. You might surprise yourself by what you have written. Maybe you will learn something new about yourself. Whatever you have discovered on this 21-day journey, treasure it, dig deep and remember to be kind to yourself.

Just because your 21 days have come to an end does not mean your newfound healing has to end. Choose a few of your favorite affirmations and recite them daily. Repeat the mantra you wrote to yourself on a consistent basis. Draw strength from your revelations and ground yourself on the desires you wish to accomplish.

HEALING LOOKS GREAT ON YOU!

Follow Isabel on Instagram for your dose of inspiration & motivation @ Instagram.com/Isabeltheauthor_

Learn more about Isabel @Isabeltheauthor.shop